RAILWAY MOODS
DEVON

ROGER MALONE

HALSGROVE

First published in Great Britain in 2005

British Library Cataloguing-in-Publication Data
A CIP record for this title is available from the British Library

ISBN 1 84114 425 8

HALSGROVE
Halsgrove House
Lower Moor Way
Tiverton, Devon EX16 6SS
Tel: 01884 243242
Fax: 01884 243325
email: sales@halsgrove.com
website: www.halsgrove.com

Printed and bound by D'Auria Industrie Grafiche Spa, Italy

INTRODUCTION

Back in the mid-fifties a small boy sat in a Dawlish teashop. While the babble from adult relatives droned about him he stared out, transfixed, at the ribbon of rail separating town from sea. Trains bustled along it with fascinating frequency.

To young eyes this summer Saturday procession had the giddy rapidity of a giant clockwork trainset. Locomotives trailing cotton-wool clouds sped eager holiday-makers to the palm-treed magnet of Torbay, or further west towards the blue waters of the Cornish Riviera. In the opposite direction they hauled people homeward; red cliffs, sandy beaches and shimmering sea soon a memory as the line curved inland, up-country and back to the daily grind.

This amazing merry-go-round of railway entertainment left an indelible image. It was one which, years later, ironically sowed the seeds for this book. Wouldn't it be great to recreate a pictorial impression of that Dawlish afternoon...

But before that thought bore any possibility of becoming a reality the railway scene was to experience a relentless transformation. Within a decade the heyday of steam was to yield to the onslaught of total dieselisation.

Steam had disappeared from the West Country by the mid-sixties with the Western Region being in almost indecent haste to rid itself of its allocation. Soon the sight of Kings and Castles, those sleek Swindon-built locomotives, hauling crack expresses was a thing of the past. Across the country the demise of the nation's steam fleet was unstoppable. With gathering momentum locomotives were being withdrawn and, save for a fortunate few, dispatched to the scrap yard.

The Southern Region soldiered on. However, although steam-hauled expresses ran from Waterloo to Weymouth and Salisbury right up to July 1967 its reign in Devon had already been relinquished. Steam had been swept away in a rising tide of modernisation – further hastened by the transfer of former Southern routes to the charge of the Western Region.

No more would West Country Class Pacifics – evocatively named after locations they served – head rakes of green coaches through the agriculturally rich Devon heartland and skirt the dramatic northern slopes of Dartmoor. Now gone were the days when, on reaching Okehampton, they swung right at Meldon Junction towards the Atlantic coast, or continued on to Plymouth via Tavistock.

But if those halcyon days had been steam's Indian summer, it was now reaching the twilight zone. In August 1968, the few remaining embers of British Rail steam glowed their last. On the Midland Region the country's final three steam sheds – Lostock Hall, Rose Grove and Carnforth – closed. This Lancastrian outpost was the final chapter in the demise of steam. An era was over.

Keen to erase all memory of this transport dinosaur British Rail imposed a total steam ban. Modernisation was

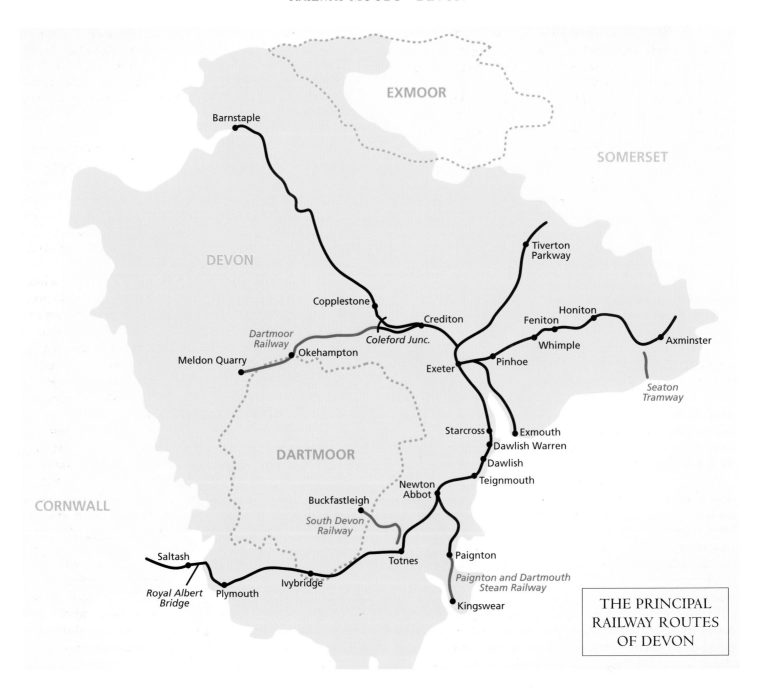

Barnstaple

EXMOOR

SOMERSET

DEVON

Tiverton
Parkway

Copplestone

Crediton

Honiton

Feniton

*Dartmoor
Railway*

Coleford Junc.

Whimple

Axminster

Meldon Quarry

Okehampton

Exeter

Pinhoe

*Seaton
Tramway*

Starcross

Exmouth

Dawlish Warren

DARTMOOR

Dawlish

Teignmouth

Newton
Abbot

Buckfastleigh

CORNWALL

*South Devon
Railway*

Totnes

Paignton

Saltash

*Paignton and Dartmouth
Steam Railway*

Ivybridge

*Royal Albert
Bridge*

Plymouth

Kingswear

THE PRINCIPAL
RAILWAY ROUTES
OF DEVON

the word. Steam was sidelined to museums and preserved railways, never to darken the network again. The only exception was occasional mainline sorties by the world-famous 'Flying Scotsman'.

Eventually the ban was lifted. It was felt enough time had passed from the end of working steam for the public to register that their rail system had long since become a smoke-free zone. There was modern traction and there was preserved steam – and there was now a cautious acceptance that there was room for both.

No longer ostracised as an outmoded, often dirty, form of transport, the glinting steam survivors basked in a born-again aura of awe. To the delight of enthusiasts steam specials began putting in occasional appearances on selected routes.

Nothing came Devon's way until the summer of 1985. That year the Western Region celebrated the 150th anniversary of the Great Western Railway. To mark the occasion a limited number of steam specials were to travel along the West of England mainline to Plymouth. And, as an added bonus, the trains would be double-headed.

For the first time in two decades Devon was roused by the triumphant exhaust beat of locomotives storming the demanding gradients of Dainton, Rattery and Hemerdon. Crowds cheered their progress and photographers jostled for the best positions.

At Dawlish well-wishers were out in droves, clustered several deep by the line-side. Enthusiasts, locals, holiday-makers, young and old were rewarded as the thorough-bred celebrities curved into view and swept majestically past their admirers. There are arguably few finer places to savour such delights. This coastal route, bookended by the charms of the Exe estuary and the Teign estuary, is a photographer's paradise.

In some ways little has changed down the years. The tide comes and goes beneath the rich, red sandstone cliffs; yelps from playing children drift up from the beach and people stroll along the sea wall savouring the liberating ozone-laden air.

With a pinch of that old theatrical suspension of disbelief and a dash of wishful thinking the years roll back. By the hocus-pocus of preservation, time blurs as, for a fleeting moment, ghosts of the fifties and sixties materialise, large as life, in the twenty-first century as if they had never faded away.

Enthusiasts muse approvingly over these action replays. Casual observers, however, many too young to appreciate these historical niceties or maybe indifferent to such comparisons anyway, simply savour the spectacle as an unexpected bonus and move on. It would be nice to think they have been touched, albeit briefly, by what they have seen. A feel-good factor born out of the romance of steam, with its proud, often percussive progress.

While photographers aim cameras at the approaching train, onlookers – unburdened by such self-inflicted pressures – often offer a friendly wave. It is always a pleasure to see such spontaneous delight – for older people a brief nudge of nostalgia, for children an exciting new spectacle. These days no schoolboy dreams of becoming an engine driver, but Thomas the Tank Engine and the family-friendly preserved railways have done much to kindle affection for the steam locomotive in a whole new generation.

Amongst adults the combined fascination with photography and railways creates an interesting hybrid, the railway photographer. Individuals span the whole spectrum from fairweather snappers to photographic fanatics. I like to imagine myself there somewhere in the middle – clearly more obsessed than a snapper but hopefully, for appearances sake if nothing else, falling short of the opposite end of the scale!

Certainly the whole business has an addictive quality to it. Even 'non-enthusiast' family members have to admit a little railway photography en route is a small price to pay for a good day out. A mouthwatering bacon buttie at the Red Rock Cafe, Dawlish Warren lingered in my daughter's memory far longer than the steam engine that roared by while she was eating it.

It is July 1985 and steam has returned. GWR 4-6-0 'Drysllwyn Castle' pilots 'Hagley Hall' at Plymouth station. Briefly sharing the limelight with them is Class 50 diesel No 50004 'St Vincent', a locomotive type which, ironically like the steam locomotives before it, has since been replaced by more modern motive power.

On another occasion a meal in the waterside pub at Cockwood Harbour after a returning special passed in golden evening light rounded off a pleasant day for us all.

Even on your own you are never at a loss for company. A camaraderie born of a shared enthusiasm bonds strangers. The way dog walkers recognise kindred spirits so railway photographers can spot like-minded camera-laden individuals a mile off. Very reassuring if you have an uneasy feeling you got the day wrong!

Long waits can be enlivened with some entertaining conversations as well as by observing occasional lineside eccentricity. I am always amused when secateurs are drawn from gadget bags and brandished at offending brambles threatening to claw their way into someone's composition.

As a rule people are about as unwanted in most railway pictures as bits of bramble – and photographers go to great lengths to keep them out. Having got a good location on the Shaldon roadbridge with nothing but water between me and the line I was guaranteed a human free shot. That was until a lone rower arrived from the far shore, beached his boat, and, to the horror of gathered photographers, climbed onto a rock between us and the approaching train. Ironically, in this case, I think he unwittingly enhanced the picture!

Once, at Cowley Bridge, Exeter the shout went up from someone with a mobile phone that the special was running fifty minutes late. One enthusiast downed tools, turned his back on the line with disdain and settled down to the long wait by reading a book. A quarter of an hour later the train suddenly appeared around the curve without warning, throwing photographers into panic. It had made up time and was now only fifteen minutes late – or thirty-five minutes early depending on your point of view. The moral of the story is don't believe everything you hear, and never take your eye off the line. Needless to say our now cursing book reader did not get his shot.

I didn't get my shots one day despite finding some delightful locations along the Exe estuary – it wasn't until after pressing the shutter several times I realised I had forgotten to put a film in the camera! That's when you need a consolatory pint in the Atmospheric Railway pub at Starcross.

Photography can be a great motivator. And, if it is in your blood, the call of steam is a better early morning wake-up call than any alarm clock. Down the years I have paid my dues on draughty platforms, windswept embankments and rain-lashed bridges.

I have also basked in brilliant sunshine – sometimes seeing that contrary orb slip behind a bank of cloud out of total perversity just as the train approaches. Unlike the contained environment of preserved railways the main line is infinitely more exciting and far less forgiving. There is just one chance to get it right.

A steam locomotive may be powering towards you at 70mph; or storming a gradient; Vesuvian smoke erupting skyward and an exhaust beat blasting like the breath of an angry dragon. And there is the buzz. Trying to freeze a moment of potent steam atmosphere on film. A visual celebration of the train in its environment. The challenge of capturing the sheer exhilaration of steam in full cry, not in a museum or corralled on a preserved railway, but unleashed and triumphantly reliving former glories on the mainline.

A day's steam chasing usually starts with me planning to go to one location and then ending up somewhere totally different. Such indecision is often driven by a touch of impending panic. You wait weeks for a special and don't want to blow your chances with a wrong decision. The weather is average at location 'A' – but will it be better or even worse at location 'B'? And if you leave it too late to change your mind and the traffic is bad you could miss the train altogether. These important dilemmas can preoccupy a desk-bound mid-week moment as the prospect of the weekend's photographic outing swims invitingly into view.

The draw of classic scenic stretches such as Dawlish and Torbay, and stiff climbs guaranteed to produce impressive locomotive performances, ensure Devon is a popular destination among enthusiasts and organisers of steam specials. And, as it is blessed with so much beautiful scenery both inland and along the coast, the railway photographer is spoilt for choice when it comes to locations.

However, while mainline steam is no stranger to the West Country it is still a far from common sight. In 2003 Devon enjoyed about a dozen steam excursions, and in 2004 the number almost reached twenty. Most of the trains' destinations divide between Plymouth and Torbay for the Paignton and Dartmouth Steam Railway. Occasionally they terminate at Exeter via the former Southern mainline from Salisbury. Steam has also made forays to Okehampton Station, now the headquarters of the Dartmoor Railway. Also, very occasionally, it continues beyond Plymouth and crosses the Tamar into Cornwall.

In the past two decades approximately thirty-five different locomotives from some twenty-seven classes have proudly crossed the county line. While Devon is traditionally the preserve of former Great Western Railway and Southern Railway locomotives, the county has also played host to steam celebrities from the other two members of the 'Big Four' – the LMS and the LNER, plus survivors from the post-nationalisation era of British Railways.

It constantly amazes me that we can still enjoy mainline steam in Devon in the twenty-first century – some 40 years after it all officially ended. Such good fortune is down to the sheer hard work of the preservation movement and the excellent good will of the network bosses.

This book is for anyone who delights in the sight of a working steam locomotive – be they enthusiast, nostalgist, or someone who simply saw one in passing and went home with their spirits a little lifted because of it.

Thanks to the on-going and varied visits by specials, I have been able to fulfil my wish of re-capturing the magic of steam at Dawlish and expand that to encompass the whole of the county. Through the images on these pages I hope to share some of the pleasure I have gained from photographing mainline steam in Devon. Where known, the date on which the photograph was taken appears at the end of each caption.

Roger Malone
2005

Sound and spectacle as two GWR 4-6-0s pound up the 1-in-122 incline towards Bittaford with their Bristol bound train. 'Hagley Hall' is the pilot locomotive.

(85)

GWRs 'Drysllwyn Castle' and 'Clun Castle' head through Exeter's Riverside Yard towards Cowley Bridge on their return run to Bristol. (9/85)

GWR superpower – 'Drysllwyn Castle' and 'Hagley Hall' make a stunning impression as they approach Exeter St Thomas station with a down special on a glorious July afternoon. (85)

'Drysllwyn Castle' and 'Hagley Hall' begin to climb the demanding Dainton bank with the Plymouth bound 'Great Western Limited'. (7/85)

The view from Shaldon Bridge – as thoroughbred steeds 'Drysllwyn Castle' and 'Hagley Hall' run along the Teign Estuary with the up 'Great Western Limited'. (7/85)

Created for express passenger service, Sir William Stanier's 'Princess Royal' Class, introduced in 1933, looks every inch an aristocrat. No 6201 'Princess Elizabeth', resplendent in LMS livery, makes a grand exit from Plymouth station. The former North Road East signal box has since been demolished. (19/10/02)

'Kinlet Hall' and 'Nunney Castle' drift into Plymouth with the 'Double Duchy' special bound for Cornwall. Can you spot the pixie on the leading locomotive? (7/4/01)

GWR Manor Class 4-6-0 No 7802 'Bradley Manor' pilots GWR Castle Class 4-6-0 No 5029 'Nunney Castle' out of Plymouth creating a spectacular smoke effect which further diffused the watery winter sunlight. (17/2/96)

GWR 4-6-0 No 7029 'Clun Castle' glints like a jewel in the early morning light as it arrives in Plymouth with empty coaching stock prior to hauling an enthusiasts' special to Truro. (6/9/85)

Plymouth station at night with BR Standard Class 4 2-6-4T No 80098 about to leave bunker-first from platform seven with a train for Exeter. (30/4/00)

The sun glints on 'King Edward l' as the GWR King Class 4-6-0 hauls its train towards Mutley tunnel.
(31/8/02)

I have a particular fondness for the Southern Pacifics. Although the lighter West Country and Battle of Britain classes regularly reached Plymouth along the former Southern main line via Okehampton and Tavistock the mighty Merchant Navy Class locomotives normally ran no further west than Exeter Central. Here Merchant Navy Class No 35028 'Clan Line' drifts along the Plym Estuary at Laira. (21/10/00)

Merchant Navy Class No 35028 'Clan Line' shows off its splendid lines as it passes the Royal Eye Infirmary on its return journey. (21/10/00)

A delightful combination was this pairing of two BR Standard Class locomotives. BR Class 4 4-6-0 No 75014 and BR 'Britannia' Class Pacific No 70000 'Britannia' departing from Plymouth. (29/4/95)

The National Trust grounds at Saltram House offer something for everyone – dog walkers, cyclists, bird watchers and… train photographers. Most people seeing me armed with camera and tripod assumed I was on the trail of some rare wader on the River Plym. They were surprised when 'King Edward I' swept into view. (9/5/98)

Plenty of atmospheric smoke from 'King Edward I' and GWR 9300 Class 2-6-0 No 7325 with 'The Devonian' at Tavistock Junction yard as they gather speed for the demands of Hemerdon bank ahead. (30/11/96)

Above: GWR 4-6-0s No 5029 'Nunney Castle' and No 5051 'Earl Bathurst' head west through the former Aller Junction and climb towards Dainton *(Right).* (29/3/02)

LNER 'V2' Class 2-6-2 No 60800 'Green Arrow' heads purposefully over the River Plym, its smoke largely obliterating the unusual outline of Sainsbury's superstore in the background. (15/5/99)

BR Class 4 No 76079 crosses the River Dart at its tidal limit at Totnes. It is on its way to Exeter with the return 'Totnes Trotter'. (12/8/01)

Heading into Newton Abbot from Paignton with 'The Newton Antelope' is 0-6-0 pannier tank 5700 Class No 9600. This was part of the special 'Newton Abbot Transport 2000' celebrations. (13/5/00)

Merchant Navy Class Pacific No 35028 'Clan Line' bathes in low October sun as it pulls away from Totnes after a water stop.
(21/10/00)

'King Edward I', hauling a long rake of chocolate and cream coaches, sweeps through the curves leaving Teignmouth behind. (14/4/01)

A rare and most welcome visitor to Devon. Looking every bit the grand lady LMS 'Coronation' Class Pacific, No 6233 'Duchess of Sutherland,' powers along the banks of the Teign en route for Plymouth. (12/10/02)

A pair of GWR 4-6-0s at Teignmouth Boat Yard – 'Nunney Castle' and 'Earl Bathurst' curve along the Teign estuary towards Newton Abbot. (29/3/02)

BR Standard Class 4 2-6-4 tank No 80098 at Shaldon Bridge with an excursion returning to Exeter. (4/00)

LMS 'Princess' Class Pacific 'Princess Elizabeth' shines like a ruby as it powers along an almost deserted Dawlish sea wall at Rockstones with Langstone Rock in the background. (19/10/02)

'The Royal Duchy' catches the low winter sun as it heads away from Dawlish behind 'King Edward I'. (25/2/95)

British Railways Standard Class 4 2-6-4T No 80098 pulls away from a stop at Dawlish Warren station. On the left are camping coaches, once a very familiar lineside feature. (4/00)

With the wide expanse of the Exe Estuary offering the delights of Devon to its passengers, 'King Edward I' speeds through Starcross hauling the Cornwall-bound 'Par King Pioneer'. (9/5/98)

An imposing view of 'Nunney Castle' hauling the 'Torbay Castle' between Starcross and Dawlish Warren.
(4/8/01)

It was so bitterly cold you almost needed anti-freeze to get the camera to work. 'Bradley Manor' looks very vulnerable as it braves the elements and hurries through Dawlish as the sea wall is pounded by powerful waves. (20/1/96)

On a much calmer day No 7802 'Bradley Manor' looks splendid as it canters along the Dawlish sea wall at Rockstones. Passengers have a wonderful view of the empty beach – but a view of the locomotive seems to be a stronger attraction judging from the heads hanging out the windows. (22/1/00)

A positive head turner – 'King Edward I' provides some dramatic black smoke effects to ensure attention as it powers along the up line just east of Dawlish. (5/9/99)

Star turn – the 'Flying Scotsman' snakes its coaches away from Teignmouth Docks as it approaches Shaldon Bridge, nearing the end of its journey with the 'Newton Abbot 2000' special. (13/5/00)

A Swindon-built pedigree if ever there was one. Having left Exeter and Cowley Bridge Junction behind, 'King Edward I' gets into its stride as it climbs the 1-in-620 gradient towards Stoke Canon with the 'Midland Devonian'. (5/9/99)

Perhaps the archetypal idea of what seaside summers should be. 'Bradley Manor' skips along the seawall towards Teignmouth basking in the sunshine and admiring glances of the onlookers. (8/03)

Sharing some of the summer duties is LMS Stanier Class 5 No 45407 – running as No 45157 'The Glasgow Highlander' – speeding its train past Cockwood Harbour towards Starcross on a Paignton-Exeter 'Dawlish Donkey' working. (8/02)

Boats and trains... GWR 4-6-0 No 6024 'King Edward I' and GWR Mogul 2-6-0 No 7325 hurry their charge past Cockwood Harbour for a water stop at Exeter St David's. (30/11/96)

'Nunney Castle' makes a splendid sight as it skirts Cockwood Harbour. (24/2/96)

LNER A4 Class Pacific 'Union of South Africa' powers along showing its sleek streamlined shape to advantage as it speeds the up 'Torbay Express' towards Teignmouth. (8/04)

Bathed in the sort of evening light every photographer loves – BR Standard Class 4 2-6-0 No 76079, seen near Powderham, sprints towards Exeter. (8/01)

Exeter bound, BR Standard Class 4 2-6-4 tank No 80079, running bunker-first, bustles its train eastwards along the banks of the Exe at Powderham. (5/4/99)

One of those golden afternoons when time seems to hang suspended and sounds drift across the water with remarkable clarity. I sat here, near Teignmouth boatyard, with my eldest daughter Zara, chatting about nothing in particular and soaking up the sunshine while we waited. 'Earl Bathurst's' progress could be seen a long way up the Teign estuary before it reached us, steadily eclipsing the calm with the quick beat of its exhaust. (8/03)

Running ahead of a thundery sky, 'Bradley Manor' heads for the coast as it lays down its own dramatic smoke clouds at Dawlish Warren. (8/03)

This busy view of Paignton station with the departing LNER A4 Pacific 'Union of South Africa' makes me smile. It reminds me of those cheery jigsaw puzzles and jaunty toytown trainsets crammed with a jumble of detail. So feast your eye on trains, including the Paignton and Dartmouth Steam Railway on the left, traffic, crossing gates, pedestrians in droves and buildings in abundance… (8/04)

So impressive did A4 Pacific 'Union of South Africa' look, simmering gently at Plymouth station, I could have admired it for hours. (22/11/03)

'King Edward I' reminds us of a time when these elegant machines, with their polished copper and brass, were part of the daily mainline scene. Here the preserved King gets set for a Plymouth departure in the dying light of a cold November afternoon. (13/11/04)

No 5051 rounds the curve at Langstone Rock – nature's contribution to the delights of train watching, offering as it does, panoramic views of this spectacular coastal section of track. (8/03)

Power and aesthetic lines combine in the mighty Stanier-designed LMS Coronation Class Pacifics. Here 'Duchess of Sutherland' can be appreciated at close quarters at Plymouth station. (27/10/01)

'Flying Scotsman' means business as it accelerates away from Exeter. (29/12/99)

Once an everyday scene – BR Standard Class 4 4-6-0 No 75014 shunts a coach at Plymouth providing much entertainment for the onlookers. (29/4/95)

LNER A2 Class Pacific 'Blue Peter' departs from Plymouth. When still owned by British Railways this locomotive visited Devon in 1966 hauling an enthusiasts' special to Exeter. (2/7/00)

It's a murky day as this unusual pairing of GWR Mogul No 7325 and LMS Mogul No 2968 ease their coaches out of Plymouth. (8/11/97)

BR Standard Class 4 No 76079 has steam to spare as it steps it out of Plymouth. (5/8/01)

A seagull's eye view of steam. Seen from Langstone Rock, 'King Edward I' speeds west along the gentle curves that hug the coastal contours of this stretch between Dawlish and Dawlish Warren. (13/11/04)

The 'Flying Scotsman' leans into the curve as it races towards Teignmouth. A woman wrote to a newspaper complaining she had taken her children to see this famous locomotive and it had been a disappointing experience. There was no smoke and it raced through the station without slowing down for the children to wave at it! (30/6/01)

The diminutive GWR Collett 1400 Class 0-4-2 tank is an unlikely contender when it comes to carrying the mantle of mainline steam. But, in what was to be the first summer season of regular trips, No 1450 showed just what small can do on the 'Dawlish Donkey' service. Having started its train at Exeter it is seen here departing from Dawlish for Newton Abbot. (4/98)

The Black Swan, Dawlish's famous emblem, is already lit up on this dull Spring afternoon as No 1450 hurries across Colonnade Viaduct. (4/98)

No 7325 pilots No 2968 as they make a workman-like display at Starcross. It was particularly pleasing when this interesting combination of GWR and LMS 2-6-0 Moguls finally curved into view. By then I had spent an age standing on a stone groin with the tide sloshing about below. That movement, combined with taking readings through the lens, gave me an involuntary nautical sway that at times threatened to dislodge me from my precarious perch. (8/11/97)

BR Standard tank No 80098 pulls away from Dawlish with the Teign Valley Wanderer. With a backdrop of beach and bay it is not hard to see why so many people are drawn to this attractive part of Devon. (4/00)

Above: It is an August summer's evening and the town's coloured lights are already on as BR Class 4 No 76079 slows for a stop at Dawlish. (8/01)

Right: 'Earl Bathurst' bursts out of Kennaway tunnel and accelerates its train along the Dawlish seafront, heading home to Bristol. (8/04)

Perhaps this is the essence of what draws railway photographers to Dawlish time and time again. Here it is – sunshine, blue sea and steam in abundance as GWR 4-6-0 'Bradley Manor' pilots BR Britannia Class Pacific No 70000 'Britannia' through this holiday town. (14/10/95)

A spectacular smoke display from West Country Class Pacific No 34016 'Bodmin' is enhanced by the angle of the evening sun. Although this is Exeter St David's, the sun-baked, somewhat unkempt track area seems more reminiscent of some dust-dry foreign location than the heart of Devon. (30/9/00)

Thomas the Tank Engine seems to have something to smile about as he enjoys his celebrity status, meeting his fans at the Exeter 150 Railfair. (5/94)

GWR 1400 Class No 1420, named 'Bulliver' and based at the South Devon Railway, puts in an appearance at the Exeter 150 Railfair.

These two classes of Southern locomotives make an impressive sight side-by-side at the Exeter 150 Railfair. On the left is un-rebuilt West Country Class Pacific No 34105 'Swanage', and on the right the more powerful Merchant Navy Class No 35005 'Canadian Pacific'. The Merchant Navies were all rebuilt with their streamlined casing removed, while some of the West Country Class remained streamlined all their working life. (5/94)

'Earl Bathurst' looks every inch a GWR pedigree locomotive as it heads west towards Tiverton Parkway. (5/9/04)

An idyllically peaceful scene as 'King Edward I' crosses Bittaford viaduct with a glimpse of the bracken-bronzed southern slopes of Dartmoor in the distance. After this the car's exhaust fell off. I had to improvise with my trouser belt in a barely successful attempt to tether the exhaust while progressing at 10mph to the nearest garage. En route it made the most awful grating noise at every bump in the road. I was pleased with the picture so, all in all, a good, if costly, trip out… (13/11/04)

To Devon and beyond – pulling away from Totnes at the foot of Rattery bank is The Penzance Pirate, headed by 'King Edward I', with plenty of steam miles ahead before reaching its Cornish destination. (19/9/98)

'Earl Bathurst' heads out of Paignton on the final leg of its journey to Kingswear. It will shortly cross over to the nearside track to gain the line owned by the Torbay and Dartmouth Railway. (9/04)

Viewed from the conveniently-positioned road bridge, 'Nunney Castle' makes sedate progress over the Royal Albert Bridge, Brunel's 1859 masterpiece. Seeing it above the rippled waters of the Tamar as it approaches Cornwall is a truly inspiring sight.

'King Edward I' approaches Devon high above Saltash Passage with 'The Eden Express'. Behind Brunel's famous railway bridge is the less elegant road bridge. (31/8/02)

The sun makes nice textures out of the drifting exhaust from BR Standard Class 5 4-6-0 No 73096 as it hurries past Rewe between Exeter and Cullompton. (15/3/03)

Bradley Manor leaves a smoke trail in its wake on a perfectly still morning at Cockwood Harbour. (16/3/96)

LNER 'V2' Class 2-6-2 'Green Arrow' brings a dash of Eastern elegance to the West of England mainline with 'The Mayflower' as it strides up the short climb from Exeter St David's station to Exeter St Thomas in the rain. (25/4/99)

'King Edward I' heads west through the Plymouth suburbs having just crossed the iron girder viaduct at Western Mill between Keyham and St Budeaux. Soon it will cross the River Tamar and enter Cornwall. (9/5/98)

Left: Super power on Hemerdon bank – Castles 'Nunney Castle' and 'Earl Bathurst' approach the summit in a crescendo of pounding exhaust beats. (21/8/04)

Below: After breaking their outward journey to take on water at Newton Abbot, 'Nunney Castle' and 'Earl Bathurst' present their admirers with a rewardingly noisy and smoky departure. To the right is the ruins of the former wagon repair shop. (21/8/04)

In mellow light LNER 'V2' Class locomotive 'Green Arrow' is homeward bound at Rewe just north of Stoke Canon. The River Culm is glimpsed in the background. (15/5/99)

No 7819 'Hinton Manor' pilots King Class 4-6-0 No 6000 'King George V' on the climb between Ivybridge and Bittaford. (27/10/85)

Once a familiar sight – a steam train threading its way through Plymouth's terraced suburbs. 'Nunney Castle' and 'Earl Bathurst' pass through Keyham station en route for Cornwall. (29/3/02)

With the delights of the seaside still ahead, Castle Class 4-6-0 No 5051 'Earl Bathurst' speeds towards Cullompton. (5/9/04)

LNER 'V2' Class 2-6-2 'Green Arrow' returns to Devon after a short visit to the Bodmin and Wenford Steam Railway. Here it rumbles off Weston Mill Viaduct on the approach to Keyham. (15/5/99)

'Earl Bathurst' slows as it prepares to stop at Newton Abbot on the return leg of the Torbay Express in what is a delightful early September evening. (5/9/04)

LMS Stanier Black Five 4-6-0s Nos 45407 and 45110 approach the outskirts of Exeter near Cowley Bridge. (15/8/99)

The two Black Fives (45407 and 45110) make good speed along the galloping grounds near Exminster en route to Plymouth. (15/8/99)

Black Five No 45407 with the earlier 'Lion and Wheel' British Railways crest on the tender, and No 45110 with the later version, haul their train away from Plymouth station past the attractive red-brick Royal Eye Infirmary building. (15/8/99)

LNER 'A4' Class Pacific 'Union of South Africa' at speed near Tiverton Parkway. It will shortly stop at Tiverton Loop – formerly Tiverton Junction – to take on water before continuing west with the down 'Torbay Express'. (8/04)

A gorse bush in full bloom provides an added splash of lineside colour as British Railways Standard Class 4 2-6-4T No 80098 hurries towards Starcross. (4/00)

A heavy downpour has just ended as BR Standard Class 2-6-0 No 76079 eases its stock into Paignton station to pick up passengers for the return run to Exeter. (8/01)

After the rain the sun has emerged just in time to give a little added sparkle to No 76079's departure. (8/02)

BR Standard Class 5 4-6-0 No 73096 means business as it heads 'The South West Standard' away from Exeter at Cowley Bridge Junction with a rousing exhaust beat. (2/10/99)

A nail-biting experience. I had always wanted to photograph a train on this bridge. There was virtually no advance warning as the 'Flying Scotsman' approached. Any sound the locomotive may have made easing down the 1 in 37 bank between Exeter Central and Exeter St David's would be almost drowned out by passing traffic. It was a case of grabbing the brief opportunity between the roofs and the tree. Luckily I got the shot I hoped for. My twin daughters Zoe and Zeta accompanied me and, with disposable cameras they received as Christmas presents, effort-lessly bagged a brace of nice pictures! Quite humbling, really … (29/12/99)

Normally day-glo is a photographic no-no. But in this crisp, low winter light I felt the offending policeman and railway official actually lent something to the shot with their bright orange jackets set against the vibrant LNER apple green of the 'Flying Scotsman'. Sorry about that … (29/12/99)

A final check before LMS Stanier 'Coronation' Class 4-6-2, No 46229 'Duchess of Hamilton' sets out from Exeter St David's for the climb up to Exeter Central and the former Southern route home. (16/11/96)

A double delight – two BR Standard Class 4 2-6-4Ts Nos 80079 and 80080 head their train away from Exeter on the up line at Cowley Bridge. (2/5/94)

BR Standard Class 4 No 76079 skirts the Plym Estuary with an excursion to Plymouth. (5/8/01)

Travelling tender first, No 76079 hastens its train past Langstone Rock. (9/8/01)

Torbay-bound Castle 'Earl Bathurst' races towards Dawlish Warren on the through lines. (8/03)

Although in the early days of British Railways some locomotives briefly carried an experimental blue livery, this locomotive was not one of them. However Merchant Navy Class Pacific No 35005 'Canadian Pacific' does look the part as it approaches Exminster. In the background is the flyover carrying the M5. (8/5/99)

It was a fortunate decision to go to Honiton Station to photograph West Country Class Pacific No 34027 'Taw Valley' with a special from Exeter. The light was poor and rain was threatening. The West Country could be heard approaching but instead of powering through the station the locomotive was halted by the signal box with a brief signal check.

Coasting through Honiton, Standard Class 4 4-6-0 No 75069 in BR lined green livery hauls two support coaches en route for Exeter. (28/6/92)

The Merchant Navy Class Pacifics were once regular performers on this former Southern mainline between Waterloo and Exeter. Here No 35028 'Clan Line' rekindles past glories as it heads west through Honiton on a rainy day. (24/3/01)

Immaculately turned out ex-LSWR 'King Arthur' Class 4-6-0 No 777 'Sir Lamiel' is an impressive sight blasting up through the remains of the former Seaton Junction. This station was once a busy junction with branch trains departing for Seaton on the coast. Now part of the former branchline trackbed is occupied by the Seaton Tramway. (6/92)

Standard Class 5 No 73096 bears down on the level crossing at Axe Gates before Axminster station with the Exeter-bound Cathedrals Express. Now a single track, this was once a double mainline with the original downline where the barriers are now. (7/11/04)

West Country Class Pacific 'Taw Valley' masquerades as No 34045 'Ottery St Mary' as it heads west at Wilmington with the Exeter bound 'Atlantic Coast Express'. (5/9/04)

BR Class 4 4-6-0 No 75069 drifts through the remains of Seaton Junction. (28/6/92)

'Sir Lamiel' gets some light servicing at Exeter Central. This was once a busy yard full of sidings. (28/6/92)

'Ottery St Mary' heads tender-first with its support coach through Exeter Central. It will travel to Yeovil Junction for servicing. The special it brought to Exeter St David's will be hauled by diesel back to Yeovil Junction where the West Country Class locomotive will once again take over. (5/9/04)

After speeding through Axminster, 'Sir Lamiel' tackles the stiff 1-in-100 climb up to Seaton Junction. (6/92)

BR Standard Class 5 No 73096 works hard as it climbs towards the summit of Honiton bank at Wilmington with an Exeter bound train. This former southern route was once a busy double track mainline. (15/3/03)

Travelling tender first to Okehampton, GWR 2-6-0 No 7325 and LMS 2-6-0 No 2968 make an attractive sight as they head towards Newton St Cyres with 'The Meldon Meanderer'. They are travelling on what was the former Southern Railway mainline to Plymouth and destinations along the Atlantic coast. (25/10/97)

A wonderful sight for all Southern enthusiasts – the first time a West Country Class Pacific has travelled along this former Southern route since the end of steam. No 34016 'Bodmin' looks spectacular with its rake of green coaches. It is seen here shortly after it has left the West of England mainline at Cowley Bridge junction. (30/9/00)

'Bodmin' halts at Crediton before pulling away over the level crossing and past the original LSWR signal box.

No 34016 'Bodmin' heads on beyond Okehampton towards the end of the line at Meldon. To the left is the site of the former Military Sidings used in the summers of 1960–1964 for the Surbiton to Okehampton car carrier service. The Dartmoor Railway, based at Okehampton, now runs trains over this line between Meldon and Sampford Courtenay.

West Country Class Pacific No 34027 'Taw Valley' heads out of Exeter Central with 'The Rougemont Limited' passing the now demolished former Exeter Central East signal box. (5/9/93)

Battle of Britain Class Pacific No 34067 'Tangmere' approaches Whimple station with the down Atlantic Coast Express. The train, which had departed from Waterloo was bound for Okehampton. 'Tangmere' was the first un-rebuilt Bulleid Pacific to traverse the former Southern mainline in Devon since the end of steam. (4/10/03)

An appreciative crowd gather at Crediton station to welcome the 'Atlantic Coast Express'. (4/10/03)

'Tangmere' departs from Crediton on the remaining part of its journey to Okehampton. (4/10/03)

'Tangmere' passes the former Southern Railway station of Sampford Courtenay en route to Okehampton. Sampford Courtenay has since been reopened as a station by the Dartmoor Railway. (4/10/03)

The former Southern Railway Okehampton station is now enjoying a fresh lease of life as a visitor centre. Here 'Tangmere' terminates the Atlantic Coast Express and takes on water.

'Tangmere' departs Exeter St David's Station with the return leg of the Atlantic Coast Express. It travelled down the southern route from Waterloo and was about to head back up the western main line to Paddington.

Hall Class 4-6-0 No 4936 'Kinlet Hall' pilots King Class 4-6-0 No 6024 'King Edward I' at Laira Junction as they head towards Tavistock Junction yard for servicing. (25/11/00)

Another steam celebrity turns on the Laira triangle – this time it is that most famous of all engines, 'Flying Scotsman'. (30/6/01)

Above: Merchant Navy Class 4-6-2 No 35005 'Canadian Pacific', in its blue period, backs down to Plymouth station. (8/5/99)

Right: Allotments have always been part of the railway scene. Here LNER A2 Pacific 'Blue Peter' No 60532 poses beside some rather neglected ones at Laira. It was turning on the Laira triangle. It is this facility which has ensured the continued presence of steam in Plymouth. The River Plym is in the background along with the now demolished Blue Circle Plymstock Cement Works. (2/7/00)

LMS Stanier Pacific 'Duchess of Sutherland' reverses out of Plymouth after having arrived with an enthusiasts' special.
(27/10/01)

Merchant Navy Class Pacific No 35028 'Clan Line', having been turned at Laira and serviced at Tavistock Junction yard, crosses the River Plym at Marsh Mills heading tender-first back to Plymouth station. (21/10/00)

In the pantheon of steam stars the sprightly GWR City Class 4-4-0 No 3440 'City of Truro' has to be an 'A' list celebrity. It is seen here near Rewe making light of its seven-coach load as it hurries 'The Ocean Mail 100' down the West of England main-line to Exeter and on to Kingswear. In 1904 this locomotive was reputed to have reached 102mph near Wellington on a Plymouth–Paddington Ocean Mail special. (8/5/04)

Bathed in sunshine 'City of Truro' approaches the delightful run along the Exe Estuary at Powderham with 'The Ocean Mail 100'. (8/5/04)

The firebox is open as 'City of Truro' prepares for a morning departure from Plymouth. It was returning to the Midlands after taking part in the opening of a new double section of main line in Cornwall. (3/12/04)

A steady departure from Plymouth as 'City of Truro' gets effortlessly into its stride. (3/12/04)

From 1985-1988 the Dart Valley Light Railway, now the South Devon Railway, had a special dispensation to run off the branch line and terminate trains at Totnes station on selected days. Here GWR 4500 Class 2-6-2T No 4555 runs around its coaches on the West of England mainline in readiness for the return journey up the branch to Buckfastleigh. This interesting manoeuvre is now history. The building of the SDR's Littlehempston Station, coupled with a footbridge spanning the River Dart, put Totnes within easy walking distance for passengers.

LMS Pacific 'Duchess of Sutherland' hauls its rake of 'blood and custard' coaches beside the Plym Estuary at Laira on the approach to Plymouth. (27/10/01)

Above and opposite: There is always a huge debate about whether the world famous 'Flying Scotsman' looks better in its LNER apple green livery or the more subdued but equally attractive Brunswick green of its British Railway days. For a season, when its mainline certificate had run out, the locomotive guested on the Torbay and Dartmouth Railway. During that period it sported the BR livery and very smart it looked too. As it climbs the 1-in-71 gradient away from Goodrington and on to drift down along the banks of the Dart near Kingswear we can make up our own minds. (8/93)

'King Edward I' passes the site of the former Plympton Goods Yard before starting to attack the taxing gradient of Hemerdon bank. (30/5/98)

Reflecting the last of the November light 'King Edward I' and GWR 2-6-0 No 7325 are about to plunge under the A377 Exeter to Crediton road at Cowley Bridge. (30/11/96)

Dusk is falling quickly as 'King Edward I' makes a dramatic departure from Plymouth on a cold winter's afternoon. 'King Edward I' has been one of the most frequent of the steam visitors to Devon in recent years. (13/11/04)

GWR Manor Class 4-6-0 'Hinton Manor', looking resplendent in early BR black livery, and GWR King Class 4-6-0 'King George V' at Laira Junction where they are about to turn on the Laira triangle. The locomotives would then set back tender-first to Plymouth station prior to hauling the 'final' Great Western Limited from Plymouth to Bristol. (27/10/85)

'Hinton Manor' pilots 'King George V' towards Bittaford near the site of the former Cantrell Sidings where interchange was once made to the incline serving the long-gone Redlake Tramway. The King, the flagship of the Great Western Railway, carries an American locomotive bell above its buffer beam which it received when exhibited in America in 1927 at the Baltimore & Ohio Railroad Centenary celebrations. (27/10/85)

BR Britannia Class Pacific No 70000 'Britannia' and BR Class 4 4-6-0 No 75014 at Plymouth station.
(29/4/95)

'Bradley Manor' and No 70000 'Britannia' breast the summit at Hemerdon bank and are about to begin the descent to Plympton on a perfect autumn day. (14/10/95)

Stanier Class 5 4-6-0 No 45407, masquerading as No 45157, sprints along the banks of the Teign Estuary.
(8/02)

Not all anoraks are dull! Some brightly coloured onlookers are here to wave as GWR 0-4-2T No 1450 skips along with the 'down' Dawlish Donkey service at Langstone Rock. (4/98)

Above: BR Standard 2-6-4 tanks Nos 80080 and 80079 ease around the curve at Cowley Bridge Junction. After arriving at Exeter St David's the locomotives separated and 'top and tailed' the train as it travelled back to the junction, swinging on to the former Southern Railway mainline *(left)*, and branching off at Coleford Junction for a trip along the Tarka route to Barnstaple. The train is seen heading towards Copplestone *(right)*. (5/94)

Enjoying a bracing run out along the coast at Dawlish are BR 2-6-4 tanks Nos 80080 and 80079. The trip was in connection with the Exeter 150 Railfair. (2/5/94)

The returning Standard tanks are seen enjoying their seaside sojourn as they hurry along at Cockwood Harbour, this time with No 80079 leading. (2/5/94)

LNER A2 Class Pacific 'Blue Peter' makes a volcanic departure as it blasts out from under Houndiscombe road bridge at Plymouth station. (2/7/00)

Above: A4 Pacific 'Union of South Africa' piles on the speed at Powderham with the up 'Torbay Express'. (8/04)

Right: 'Union of South Africa' leaves Dawlish Warren viewed from the photographic eyrie of Langstone Rock. It was followed minutes later by a cloud burst that gave me a good soaking. On a fine day the Red Rock snack bar below is a great place for steam – and alfresco bacon butties!

(8/04)

LMS Coronation Class Pacific 'Duchess of Sutherland' at Plymouth.
(27/10/01)

The powerful elegance of a Stanier Princess Royal Pacific can be fully appreciated in this view of No 6201 'Princess Elizabeth' as it drifts down from Mutley tunnel to Plymouth station. (19/10/02)

Sun, sand... and sea mist. GWR 0-6-0 tank No 9600 climbs up the bank between Paignton and Torquay near Hollicombe as it heads inland from the coast for Newton Abbot. (13/5/00)